Cocktail Party Nibbles

Helen O'Leary

David & Charles

Newton Abbot   London   North Pomfret (Vt)

For Joy

British Library Cataloguing in Publication Data

O'Leary, Helen
   Cocktail party nibbles.
   I. Snack foods   2. Entertaining
   I. Title
   641.5'68   TX740

ISBN 0-7153-8643-3

Line illustrations by Mona Thorogood

© Text: Helen O'Leary 1984
© Line illustrations: David & Charles 1984

Photoset by Typesetters (Birmingham) Ltd,
Smethwick, West Midlands
and printed in Great Britain
by A. Wheaton & Co Ltd,
for David & Charles (Publishers) Limited
Brunel House   Newton Abbot   Devon

Published in the United States of America
by David & Charles Inc
North Pomfret   Vermont 05053   USA

Contents

Acknowledgements

My very special thanks to Daphne Broadhead who first suggested *Nibbles*.

Thanks also to Anna Le Cornu whose wonderful food inspired me to research and collect the material for this book, to all the cookery writers I've ever read past and present, and to the many kind friends and my family who generously contributed recipes and ideas.

Finally my thanks to Frances who typed on and on . . . until the end.

1. Party Plans

Party Politics

Damp sausage rolls and dull dips cast an air of doom and gloom on any party. Like running dry of drink, both are guaranteed to drive your best friends home, or straight to the nearest pub, in a state of deep depression.

On the other hand, a *good* cocktail party, with plenty of interesting nibbles and sufficient drink, is the one sure way to win points on the popularity polls and to get asked back to lots yourself. Gaining a reputation as a 'great party giver' is even better.

The point is, people like being invited out. Feeling wanted adds zip and sparkle to their working day. So, if your life needs a whiff of romance, or your spirits a lift, read on and give the best cocktail party of the season yourself. This book has been compiled to help you cater for the crowds, avoid the worse pitfalls and have fun.

For a start, let me assure you there is no need to rob a bank or sell your soul to give a successful party. You don't have to be a cordon bleu cook or a lady of leisure, with hours to spare, to provide super eats, either. The best cocktail parties are frequently given by the busiest people, often on the leanest of means, without the advantage of cookery classes. The secret lies in *lists*, because with parties, as with life, a good list can save you time, temper and tears.

The trouble is, most of us are not keen on being organised, particularly in our private lives. Lists and plans sound dull and fit uneasily into the glossy party image, but both are fundamental to success and neither need be that burdensome.

Basically, only three ingredients are essential for a successful party: good food, plenty of drink and a reasonable selection of interesting people. Here's my recipe for speedy action on the party front to help you achieve all three, hassle-free.

The Party Date

Decide the time, date, place, numbers, etc. Write everything down in a spiral notebook. Keep it with you and resolve to update it daily. The trick, in the first instance, is to work out a loose plan, one sufficiently flexible to allow for alterations without causing major chaos.

Guest List

Aim for a meticulous mix of people. We keep three lists: teetotallers, drinkers and 'fish'. All our best friends are 'fish'. Here's an attempt to help you plan. Include your best friends – that goes without saying – but also include your worst enemies; it may only be you who dislikes them. Several unattached males and females – you are not running a Darby and Joan Club. The neighbours – they probably won't come but at least they have been warned and are thus less likely to complain about noise. A couple of stimulating, clashing personalities – sparks add sparkle to any party. A few beautiful people – ask them to come early, you want them to be *seen*. At least one good listener. People to avoid inviting are: bores who bang on; man-eating females – they alienate every other woman in the room – and elderly relatives, however dear, who need to sit down.

Here's the exception that proves the rule: we once gave a party for all the people we owed hospitality but liked least. They had a ball. We sat in the kitchen. The evening was apparently a wild success.

Drinks

If you want to stay solvent, it is imperative to work to a budget. Plenty of drinkable plonk is infinitely preferable to rationed thimblefuls of fine wines or expensive spirits. Unless you can afford to employ experienced, professional staff to help you, decide on one or two simple mixtures which can be served from jugs (attempting to measure, stir, shake and serve individual drinks unaided is a recipe for disaster). Co-opt a couple of good friends to help keep the jugs filled and glasses topped up. Check their willingness to help in advance.

Recipes for sophisticated cocktails number a legion. However, exorbitantly expensive concoctions decked with paper parasols and plastic swizzle-sticks may be fun to sip in smart restaurants, but they're impossible to organise for crowds, should you wish (in a moment of weakness) so to do.

Our solution to the cocktail craze is Buck's Fizz – traditionally champagne (fizzy white wine in our case), fresh orange juice with a dash of brandy in the first sugar-frosted glass. You may prefer Black Velvet (champagne and Guinness), Pimms, Harvey Wallbanger, or whatever is the current 'in' drink on your social scene.

The point is that success lies not in the trimmings, but in choosing one or at most two, easy-to-serve, popular mixtures, relevant to the temperature and time of the year.

What is even more important is that you allow your guests the freedom to imbibe as much or as little (equally important) as they wish. Pressing, over-generosity is tedious, however well meant. Meanness, on the other hand, is tantamount to disaster.

The following data may help you steer a straight course on the drinks front:

Most reputable wine merchants deal on a sale or return basis (full, sealed bottles only). Thus, over-estimating your needs can do no harm. Remember to provide mineral water, soft drinks and proper Coca-Cola for the non-drinkers.

Glasses: Paris goblets and sometimes tulip flutes are available on loan from your wine merchant – another good reason for patronising the small shop-keeper rather than the supermarket.

An average wine glass holds 142ml (5fl oz).

A typical bottle of wine contains 70cl (26fl oz) or 5–6 glasses.

A litre-sized bottle of wine contains 95cl (25.18fl oz) 6–8 glasses.

A magnum of champagne contains 145cl (54fl oz) or 10–12 glasses.

Public houses squeeze 32 single measures from a 75cl bottle of spirits.

Finally, don't fuss if drinking seems fairly brisk in the early stages – even the 'fish' slow down eventually.

The Food

The provision of bite-sized, light, nourishing, relatively non-fattening nibbles is an essential ingredient for a successful cocktail party. Good eats help keep the conversation flowing and the guests upright. Handing round a dish of delicious goodies also provides shy newcomers with an opportunity to mix. Your chosen selection need not be vast but the food offered must be fresh, appetising and easy to eat – preferably of the non-drip variety. Allow eight to ten nibbles per head, of which at least half should be reasonably substantial (ie provide blotting-paper!).

Kitchen Equipment

A certain amount of kitchen equipment is essential to produce any type of party nibble other than the store-cupboard variety. However, while it is true to say the right tool for the right job can save hours of time, it is also true that many 'labour-saving' gadgets currently in the shops are no such thing. They're labour-intensive. (Just finding the garlic press in a crowded drawer drives me insane, never mind the washing-up later.)

Good cooks rely on very few tools indeed. Here is a short list of all you need to make excellent party food.

Cook's knife:	The best you can afford. Keep a cork on the tip to preserve the point.
Chopping board:	Saves mess and looks attractive. It can also be used to serve a selection of cold meats or assorted cheeses.
Tin opener	
Icing set:	For piping fillings into dates, prunes, etc.
Cling film	
Silver foil	

And, most important, a food processor. It is an expensive item but saves hours of chopping, slicing, mincing or grating. It makes savoury butters, dips, pâtés and spreads in seconds, and at the flick of a switch produces excellent batter, pastry and choux paste *every* time. So if you don't own one already, start saving *now*.

Work Schedule

Consider first the amount of time at your disposal, then list and slot in every job. Eliminate anything which requires last-minute attention. Acknowledge your limitations and allow for your weaknesses. Resist the temptation to achieve the impossible milk-and-honey standards of television commercials (few people live in an Ideal Home situation).

Remember to allocate time to 'slow down' and 'dress up' before the party. Feeling cool, calm and confident is an essential part of party politics; so is looking good.

Serving and Presentation

When you have invested precious time and money preparing party food, it is worth paying attention to the presentation. By that I do not suggest you spend hours fussing over radish roses. The art of serving nibbles lies not so much in elaborate garnish, more in plain common sense and an eye for detail.

A few pointers . . .

Before the party arrange food on several small plates or dishes. Offer only one or two at a time (dependent on guest numbers). Switch empty or half-filled plates with replacements from the kitchen. Being urged to choose food from a 'picked-over' plate is awful; the smoked salmon has always long gone. And attempting to remove and replenish huge platters which quickly become tatty is both disruptive and time-wasting.

Food looks best on simple blue and white china plates or in shallow wicker baskets lined with apple green napkins. You may prefer silver salvers (remember to line them against acid foods), stainless-steel dishes, foil-covered trays or biscuit-tin lids. Whatever you choose, it is important to make your food look fresh and appetising. *Warning*: Avoid containers that are too precious or too heavy.

There is nothing like an electric hotplate, or tray, to keep hot nibbles 'hot' without spoiling. Beg, borrow or buy one for Christmas and mid-winter parties.

Encourage guests to circulate; place secondary nibbles – nuts, crisps, pretzels, etc – in small dishes at strategic points about the room.

Distribute ashtrays liberally throughout the party areas. Not just for ash and cigarette ends, they also prove convenient receptacles in which to deposit cocktail sticks.

Resist the urge to over-garnish. If decorate you must, restrict your efforts to the edible variety – sprigs of watercress, quarters of tomato, wedges of lemon or whole radishes.

Final Thought

Good friends number among your most valuable assets, so they deserve your best attention. Concentrate on making them feel cherished the minute they walk in the door. Be kind to their clothes – provide hangers and a rail for their coats. Put a pile of fluffy towels, good soap, hairspray and safety pins in the bathroom. Keep a box of first aid dressings and female supplies in an accessible drawer in case of emergencies. Make sure there is plenty of loo paper available in the loo – it is no use buried in the store cupboard. Remember, a *big smile* makes you look pretty and your guests feel welcome. Have fun!

2. No-nonsense Nibbles

Instant Nibbles

The sad fact is that many interesting nibbles are labour inten-
sive. And it's no secret that the thought of providing party
food unexpectedly can unnerve even experienced cooks. Yet
knowing how to deal with the situation is more a question of
getting to grips with your fears than finding time to cope in
the kitchen. Agonising over your predicament is both unpro-
ductive and time wasting.

In a real emergency, dress first, then put out the drinks
(shows guests they are expected), then organise the nibbles
(people don't mind waiting for food). Search the store-
cupboard, forage in the fridge, or raid the kids' lunch-boxes.
Offer the resulting miscellany of nuts, crisps or cubes of
cheese with a serene smile.

If emergencies are a common occurrence in your house,
here's a list of supplies you might like to keep in reserve:

Nuts: Almonds, walnuts, pecans, cobs – bought from a good
    health food shop. Store in a glass screw-top jar. If you have
    time, fry in hot butter and toss, while still warm, in salt,
    paprika or curry powder.
Olives: Black: usually in tins; green: stuffed with pimento;
    green: pitted. Olives can be bought loose from some
    delicatessen shops or from supermarkets. Once opened
    the bottled variety will keep for a few weeks in the fridge.
Gherkins: Buy with the olives.
Onions: The tiny white variety sold in glass screw-top jars.
Bottled gulls' eggs: Usually contain five eggs. Once opened
    best consumed immediately.
Tins of prawns/pâté/lumpfish etc.
Jar of Hellmann's mayonnaise. You won't fool anyone, but it's
    better than most.
Selection of: Crisps, pretzels, salty biscuits. The best come
    from that famous underwear shop. Store in an airtight tin

hidden away from flatmates, husbands or kids' prying fingers.

Rich readers or Middle Eastern commuters might also consider storing real caviar under wraps in the fridge. The perfect party food, it is instant, impressive, nourishing and non-fattening. (A friend once took Maria Callas to lunch and she ate only caviar, with a spoon and no toast!) Serve the real thing on cracked ice with toast and tots of vodka. Any other reference to the word caviar in this book refers to the poor man's variety – black lumpfish roe or red cod's roe.

Quick Cook's Nibbles

The American idea of 'mix and serve' has been accepted for years when applied to alcoholic drinks. Were it necessary to marinate, reduce, sauté and sauce a Martini, few would drink and no one would be daft enough to give cocktail parties.

But the concept can equally well be applied to food. Our supermarkets are full of wonderful foods all eagerly waiting to be tried. The following are a few suggestions. Most are based on the mix and serve principle, and all can be prepared in a few minutes with minimum fuss.

Bake Honey Sausages: dribble a tablespoon of honey over cocktail-size sausages. Cook in a pre-heated oven, 180°C (350°F) Gas 4, for 30 minutes.

Stuff pitted olives or grapes with a mixture of mock caviar and cream cheese.

Cut away the top skin from a small whole Brie, sprinkle with slivered almonds and warm in a medium oven until runny. Provide biscuits and knives for guests to help themselves.

Soak pitted dates in a little brandy. Stuff with a mixture of cream cheese mixed with a dash of horseradish.

Drain a tin of baby artichoke hearts. Spoon lumpfish into the depressions and top with a blob of sour cream.

Spread mustard over thinly sliced roast beef. Cut meat into suitable strips and wrap round small dill pickles. Secure with cocktail picks.

Mash Roquefort (or other blue cheese) to a paste and use to sandwich together the flat sides of pecan nuts.

Wrap Parma ham round cubes of melon or pawpaw. Impale on sticks.

Prepare mini uncooked kebabs. Thread cubes of green pepper, red pepper, cucumber, avocado (dipped in lemon to prevent discolouration) and orange on cocktail sticks.

Make cream cheese balls. Use 1 packet of cream cheese, add 1tbsp sour cream and add the flavour of your choice: 2tsp anchovy paste; 2tsp tomato paste; ½tsp curry powder. Form into balls and roll in finely chopped chives or almonds. Refrigerate.

Buy Melba toast from your delicatessen. Spread toasts with tomato ketchup, cover with a slice of salami and top with a piece of Mozzarella cheese. Cook for 5 minutes *only* in a pre-heated oven, 200°C (400°F) Gas 6. Watch out – these burn very easily.

Grill a selection of bacon bites. Stretch slices of streaky bacon with a knife. Divide in three. Grill until transparent. Wrap around stoned dates, prunes, pineapple chunks, maraschino cherries or grilled chicken liver. Return to grill for 2–3 minutes. Serve warm.

Stuff mushroom caps with mashed liver pâté. Top with crumbled bacon.

Make poppy seed sticks – easy, different, and great for non-cooks! Trim the crusts from slices of bread, butter each slice and cut into 3 fingers. Sprinkle liberally with poppy seeds and season with salt. Brown in a pre-heated oven, 220°C (425°F) Gas 7 for about 8 minutes.

For less hassle but more expenditure provide:

Smoked salmon on fingers of brown bread and butter: 100g (4oz) smoked salmon covers 4 slices of bread. Cut each slice into 4 fingers, sprinkle with black pepper and a splash of lemon juice.

A platter of assorted sliced salamis with radishes.

A selection of cheeses with salty biscuits.

Professionally frozen battered mushrooms, fish or chicken pieces with a mayonnaise-based dip. These only need heating in a hot oven. Follow the instructions on the packet. Buy only the very best brands – cheaper varieties tend to be mostly batter.

13

3. Canapés and Canapé Offshoots

The word canapé (meaning sofa in French) sounds grand, but is in fact nothing more frightening or complicated than a mini open sandwich.

Canapés consist of three parts: the base, a savoury butter or spread, and decorative topping.

Traditionalists insist on a toasted or croûton base. However, perfectly acceptable canapés can be made with any of the ready-to-use packaged breads – pumpernickel, pitta or rye, for example – savoury biscuits, Melba toast and pastry cases. Look for the little pastry cases in an up-market delicatessen (be warned – they are quite expensive). Two types are currently available, one from Sweden, the other from Holland.

All canapé bases other than those made from untoasted bread should be crisp. If biscuits or pastry cases have lost their 'bounce', place in a pre-heated oven, 180°C (350°F) Gas 4, for 10 minutes.

Here are three suggestions for easy, inexpensive bases to organise at home:

Slice a French loaf into rounds 6mm (¼in) thick. Spread each slice with softened butter, then top as required.

Stamp out rounds of white or brown sliced bread. Use a pastry cutter 40mm (1½in) in diameter, or coffee cup. Butter and top.

Make oven croûtons from sliced bread. Generously butter a baking tin and 'toast' suitably shaped cut-outs of white bread in a pre-heated oven, 230°C (450°F) Gas 8, for about 8 minutes. Turn once.

The following are three ideas from Denmark for non-farinaceous canapés.

Sliced waxy boiled potatoes. Top with pickled herring, dill and a blob of sour cream.

Sliced cheese (use Gouda or Edam but avoid crumbly types, ie Cheshire). Top with sliced cucumber and radish rounds.

Thick cucumber slices. Top with rounds of hard-boiled eggs and a little caviar.

Savoury Butters

Savoury butters anchor toppings and prevent bases from becoming soggy. If sufficiently smooth, and you have time to spare, they may also be piped on top of canapés for decoration. Make butters ahead of time and store in a cool place to allow flavours to develop. Spread at room temperature. Ready-baked pastry cases must be brushed out with melted butter prior to filling.

Here are a few of my favourite flavours: with 100g (4oz) unsalted butter, blend or process one of the following ingredients. Season as required.

Almond:	50g (2oz) finely chopped, blanched almonds plus juice and zest of ½ orange.
Anchovy:	4 anchovies, previously soaked in milk, mashed.
Blue cheese:	50g (2oz) blue cheese – Stilton is best.
Curry:	2tsp curry powder.
Green:	50g (2oz) chopped watercress or chives.
Maître d'hotel:	2tsp chopped parsley, squeeze of lemon, ½tsp powdered mustard.
Pimento:	2tbsp mashed tinned red pepper.
Prawn:	50g (2oz) cooked peeled prawns.
Saffron:	2tsp saffron.

Cream Cheese Spreads

These perform the same function as savoury butters. Simply mix 100g (4oz) cream cheese with one of the following flavours:

Anchovy:	2tsp anchovy paste.
Chive:	2tsp chopped watercress, 2tsp chives, ½tsp grated onion.
Fruit:	2tbsp finely chopped peach or pear.
Smoked salmon:	50g (2oz) smoked salmon, puréed, plus lemon juice to taste.

Tuna:	2tbsp mashed tuna mixed with dash of vinegar or 1tbsp mayonnaise.
Walnut:	50g (2oz) finely chopped walnuts.

Toppings

Possible toppings for canapés stretch as far as your imagination allows. It's the combination of colour and texture that counts. Listed below are some ideas for you to try. The final choice depends on your pocket or what is in your fridge at the time.

Wafer-thin slices of beef spread with mustard and topped with half a grape.

Pounded prawns or pink smoked trout, decorated with small canned green asparagus tips and slivers of red pepper.

Crab meat creamed with mayonnaise and decorated with slices of black olive.

Very small whole fish (tiny sardines, whitebait or whole prawns), plus a fine small segment of lemon or orange.

Diced ham mixed with mango chutney. Sprinkle with grated coconut.

Raw minced steak (steak tartar) with diced onions and capers.

Italian salamis topped with gherkin.

Smoked salmon with black 'caviar'.

When you prepare canapés for crowds collect together the necessary equipment and ingredients. Set up a mini production line and bribe a friend/husband/offspring to help.

If you use a bread base, many of the above may be partly prepared in advance and frozen. Remove from the freezer 2 hours before serving time.

Warning: Do *not* freeze canapés for which you have used mayonnaise (it may turn black and separate). Likewise, avoid freezing canapés for which tinned fish, defrosted fish or fleshy fruits have been used. All decoration is best done on 'the day'.

Almond Butter and Swiss Cheese Canapé
Makes 32

100g (4oz) butter
100g (4oz) almonds, finely chopped

2tsp zest of orange
2tsp orange juice
225g (8oz) Gruyère cheese, sliced
16 slices pumpernickel, halved
1 whole orange
Watercress

1. Pound together butter, almonds, orange juice and zest.
2. Spread pumpernickel slices with orange/almond butter.
3. Top each slice with Gruyère cheese cut to size. Pipe on a further swirl of almond butter. Finish with a speck of skinless orange segment and a watercress leaf.

Hot Cheese and Anchovy Canapé
Makes 20

5 slices white bread
50g (2oz) butter
2tbsp oil
100g (4oz) Bel Paese cheese, sliced
10 anchovy fillets

1. Cut bread into quarters.
2. Melt butter with oil. Fry bread until golden.
3. Cut cheese slices to fit croûton quarters. Flash under grill until cheese melts.
4. Top each croûton with ½ anchovy fillet.

Quail's Egg Mouthfuls
Makes 12

Positively the last word on canapés – expensive, time-consuming, but delicious – and best made in the morning before the party.

12 brown bread circles 5cm (2in)
100g (4oz) butter
175g (6oz) smoked salmon
12 poached quail's eggs – trim edges
50g (2oz) piped savoury butter

1. Top buttered brown bread base with slice of smoked salmon followed by poached quail's egg.
2. Pipe thin border of butter round edge of quail's egg.

Canapé Offshoots

Asparagus rolls, pinwheel sandwiches and sandwich stacks take time to prepare, but they can be made weeks ahead and stored in the freezer until required.

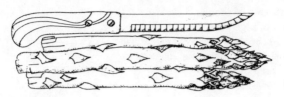

Asparagus Rolls
Makes 24

450g (1lb) canned green asparagus tips, drained
1 small uncut brown loaf (day-old bread is best)
225g (8oz) butter

1. Remove crusts from the bread. Slice in the usual way and butter.
2. Place an asparagus spear on the edge of each slice and roll up like a Swiss roll. Cut each roll in three.
3. Pack overwrapped with freezer paper in a rigid container. Store in freezer for up to one month.

Smoked Salmon Pinwheels
Makes 4 or 5 uncut pinwheels – each cuts into 4–5 slices

1 small uncut brown loaf
175g (6oz) butter
50g (2oz) cream cheese
225g (8oz) smoked salmon
Black pepper
Lemon juice

1. Trim crusts from loaf and slice lengthwise.
2. Blend together the butter and cream cheese and spread on
   bread. Cover with slices of smoked salmon. Season with ground black pepper and squeeze of lemon juice.
3. Roll up each slice of bread like a Swiss roll. Do not slice.
4. Wrap in foil or cling film and store in rigid container in freezer.
5. Defrost. When required, thaw for about 5 hours. Slice pinwheels halfway through thawing period. Be sure to use a very sharp knife.

Note: If you can't cut a straight slice of bread for love or money, try slipping the loaf in your freezer for a few minutes first. Real duffers make asparagus rolls with commercially sliced bread – the thinnest to be found.

You can always use red caviar instead of smoked salmon, to make red caviar rolls.

Here are some other fillings for pinwheel sandwiches. Quantities are sufficient for one small brown loaf.

Cheese, chive and lime
225g (8oz) cream cheese
2tbsp chives, finely chopped
2tbsp zest of lime
ltbsp lime juice
Combine all ingredients. Season to taste.

Hazelnut and chicken
100g (4oz) cooked chicken, minced
100g (4oz) hazelnuts, toasted, skinned and crushed
2tbsp double cream
Pinch of nutmeg
Combine all ingredients. Season to taste.

Tomato curry
225g (8oz) cream cheese
2tsp tomato purée
ltsp curry paste
½tbsp lemon juice
Combine all ingredients. Blend until smooth.

Parsley, beef and garlic
100g (4oz) cooked beef, finely minced
100g (4oz) parsley, finely chopped
I clove garlic, crushed
2tbsp thick homemade mayonnaise
Mix all ingredients together.

Pretty Victorian Sandwiches

Originally a tea-time treat when the ladies were 'at home' to friends, but far too good to be forgotten. Make a selection in mini-minor sizes. Use brown and white bread. Quantities given will fill one small loaf, which will make 32 small sandwiches.

Celery Walnut Sandwich

Best made with a fancy bread, eg malt loaf.

175g (6oz) celery, finely grated
ltbsp double cream
Salt
Pepper
2tsp lemon juice

Walnut butter:
100g (4oz) walnuts, finely chopped
100g (4oz) butter, softened
1/2tsp ground cinnamon
1/2tsp caster sugar
Salt
Pepper

1. Mix together filling ingredients.
2. Blend walnut butter ingredients until smooth.
3. Spread butter mixture over bread slices. Sandwich together and trim.

Queen Adelaide's Sandwich

100g (4oz) cooked tongue, minced
100g (4oz) cooked chicken, minced
2tbsp double cream
Salt
Pepper

Curry butter:
100g (4oz) butter, softened
2tsp curry paste
Itsp lemon juice
2tsp apricot jam

1. Mix together the chicken, tongue and cream. Season. Do not let the mixture become too wet.
2. Blend the curry butter ingredients together until smooth.
3. Butter thin slices of crustless bread.
4. Sandwich together buttered slices of bread with a good layer of the chicken and tongue filling. Slice into triangles. Garnish with sprigs of watercress.

Finnan Haddock Sandwich

300g (12oz) Finnan haddock, cooked and flaked
3tbsp thick lemon mayonnaise

Watercress butter:
100g (4oz) butter, softened
1 big bunch watercress (leaves only), finely chopped
Salt
Pepper

1. Mix fish with mayonnaise. Taste and season if required.
2. Blend watercress with butter. Season.

3. Butter sliced bread. Make up sandwiches. Cut into pretty shapes.

Note: Golden cutlets or smoked cod fillet may be more readily available in your shops. Either make excellent fillings.

Black and White Brick Stack
Cuts into 24 small squares

100g (4oz) Roquefort cheese or Stilton
100g (4oz) butter
225g (8oz) packet sliced pumpernickel

1. Pound together the cheese and butter.
2. Spread slices of pumpernickel with the cheese mixture and stack.
3. Wrap in foil and chill, covered with a heavy weight.
4. Slice stack thinly, divide each slice in two. Serve with a dish of radishes. Best made the night before the party.

4. Dips and Dunks

The reason why sour cream and packet onion soup mix has stayed a firm favourite for so long is because it's absolutely reliable, dead easy to prepare and not at all bad.

Sour cream remains a marvellous base for a variety of dips, but with a food processor the same consistently good results can be obtained using mayonnaise, smoothed cottage cheese, cream cheese, or savoury butters – speed, ease and variety at the flick of a switch. Use the recipes in this section as a guide. Chop and change the flavours or even the base to suit your mood. However, there is one hard and fast rule: the consistency of any dip should be such that it may be easily scooped into a dunk without dripping over clothes and carpet.

When it comes to choosing dunks, let your imagination run wild – dare to be different. A selection of interesting and different fruit and vegetables can be a joy to look at and a pleasure to eat. On the other hand, gnarled carrots and stringy celery disappoint even conscientious slimmers.

So choose sprigs of fresh green broccoli, strips of fennel, courgettes, cauliflower florets, mini corn on the cob (they come from Thailand), slices of mango, pawpaw, endive leaves, fresh dates, lychees, big succulent strawberries (if they're in season or you feel rich), mushroom caps, mange tout (blanched), green beans – Americans and Australians have no inhibitions about serving mixtures of fresh fruit and vegetables. Why we in the UK have insisted on keeping the two apart is a mystery. Skinnybins, slimmers and over-lunched executives will certainly approve. Be generous. Some people nibble the naked dunks all through the party.

Spiced Vegetables

Not necessarily the best dunk, but a winner with sophisticated slimmers. Make ahead of time; it keeps for 2–3 days in the fridge.

1 head of cauliflower, split into florets
1 celery heart, split into 7.5cm (3in) sticks

New carrots, peeled and sliced into 7.5cm (3in) strips
225g (8oz) mange tout, blanched
225g (8oz) mushroom caps, wiped clean
2 cloves garlic, chopped
ltbsp salt
715ml (1¾pt) water
142ml (¼pt) white wine vinegar
ltbsp mixed pickling spice
ltsp whole dill seeds and mustard seeds

1. Place vegetables in a glass or china bowl with garlic and salt.
2. Combine water, vinegar and seasonings. Bring to the boil. Pour mixture over vegetables.
3. Cool, then cover and marinate in fridge for a few days.
4. Drain away brine. Pat dry with kitchen towel. Arrange vegetables on a dish.

Almond Dip
Makes approximately 430ml (¾pt) in 10 seconds exactly

12 almonds, blanched and skinned
4 shallots
2tbsp mixed sweet pickle
12 pimento-stuffed olives
2 cartons natural yoghourt (142ml/5fl oz each)
1 carton sour cream (142ml/5fl oz)
Salt
Pepper
ltbsp chives

1. Process nuts, pickles, shallots and 6 olives together for 5 seconds.

23

2. Add yoghourt, sour cream and seasonings. Process for a further 5 seconds.
3. Transfer to dish and refrigerate overnight to allow flavours to blend together. Serve in a mound with chives and remaining 6 olives.

Anchovy Dip
Makes almost 275ml (½pt)

225g (8oz) cream cheese at room temperature
50g (2oz) capers, drained
50g (2oz) anchovy paste
3tbsp lager or light ale

1. Blend all ingredients together until smooth. Thin with a little more lager if too stiff.
2. Serve with square crisps or tortilla chips.

Armenian Yoghourt Dip
Makes 142ml (¼pt)

Alter proportions to suit your taste. In Turkey 3 cloves of garlic are considered minimal.

1 carton natural yoghourt (142ml/5fl oz)
¼tsp curry powder
¼tsp cumin powder
¼ clove garlic, crushed
1tsp lemon juice
Salt
Pepper

Blend or process all ingredients together. Cover and allow to stand for at least 1 hour.

Note: Traditionally, this dip is served with crisp courgette frites. (Cut courgettes in 7.5cm (3in) strips. Toss in flour. Deep-fry until crisp. Drain. Serve warm.)

Avocado and Fresh Tomato Dip
Makes 142ml (¼pt)

2 ripe avocados
2tbsp lemon juice
2tbsp wine vinegar
1 large tomato peeled, deseeded and pulped
½tsp sugar
1tsp Worcestershire sauce
½tsp Tabasco sauce

Salt
Pepper

1. Peel and stone avocados. Purée flesh with lemon juice and vinegar.
2. Add remaining ingredients. Cover and chill. Serve with fresh crudités or spiced vegetables (see p22).

Hot Cheese Dip
Makes 275ml (½pt)

225g (8oz) strong Cheddar cheese, grated
1tbsp flour
2tsp mustard powder
25g (1oz) butter
2 egg yolks, beaten
142ml (5fl oz) Guinness
Salt
Pepper

1. Combine the cheese, flour, mustard and seasonings. Melt butter in a heavy pan. Remove from heat and blend in dry ingredients.
2. Gradually add Guinness to cheese and butter mixture. Cook over high heat until thick.
3. Remove from heat. Beat in egg yolks.
4. Just before serving, gently warm mixture. Obliterate any lumps. Serve with warm canned cocktail sausages (heat them in the can).

Hot Chilli Dip
Makes approximately 1.25 litres (2pt)

An American idea for Halloween. You can make your own instant variety of chilli sauce by whisking together 2tsp Tabasco sauce and 225g (8oz) tomato pulp.

450g (1lb) steak, minced
225g (8oz) canned chilli sauce
1½tsp chilli powder
½ packet dried onion soup
½ packet dried mushroom soup
2 cartons sour cream (142ml/5fl oz each)

1. Brown beef in a heavy frying pan. Drain off excess fat.
2. Mix beef with remaining ingredients. Heat through but do not boil.
3. Serve warm with crackers, toast or tortilla (see p60).

25

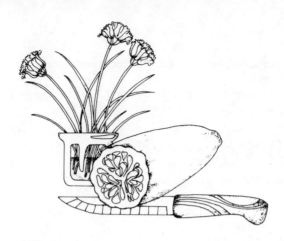

Cucumber Dip
Makes approximately 575ml (1pt)

Delicious with smoked salmon rolls if you're feeling rich.

2 fat cucumbers, peeled
2 cartons sour cream (142ml/5fl oz each)
3tbsp white wine vinegar
2tsp chives
¼tsp Tabasco sauce

1. Deseed cucumber and chop roughly.
2. Whirl all ingredients in blender or food processor.
3. Pour into serving bowl and chill.
4. Serve surrounded with rolled bite-sized nibbles of smoked salmon impaled on sticks or, less expensive, mini smoked salmon and brown bread rolls (for method, see Asparagus Rolls, p18).

Curry Cheese Dip
Makes 275ml (½pt)

225g (8oz) Dutch cheese, grated
225g (8oz) cottage cheese
1tsp curry powder
2tbsp mango chutney
1tbsp brandy
2 spring onions, chopped
Salt
Pepper

Combine all the ingredients together. Blend, process or pound until smooth. Serve with celery and cucumber sticks.

Prawn and Ginger Cream Cheese
Makes approximately 425ml (3/4pt)

225g (8oz) prawns, peeled
100g (4oz) cream cheese
142ml (5fl oz) double cream
2tbsp lemon juice
1/2tsp ground ginger, 1tsp chives

Roughly chop prawns. Blend or process until fine. Add remaining ingredients and process to combine. Serve with salty crackers.

Quick Curry Dip
Makes just under 275ml (1/2pt)

250ml (8fl oz) mayonnaise
1tsp each creamed horseradish, white vinegar, curry paste
Cayenne pepper

1. Combine all the ingredients together. Process to a smooth cream.
2. Transfer to a serving dish. Chill. Serve with cubed pineapple, strips of coconut and cucumber.

Tapenade
Makes 425ml (3/4pt)

The old Provençal word *tapenes* means 'capers', an essential ingredient in the recipe. Traditionally, tapenade took hours to make by hand, but with a blender or food processor you can make it in minutes.

275g (10oz) black olives, pitted
2tbsp each oil, lemon juice, brandy
100g (4oz) canned tuna fish, drained and flaked
75g (3oz) capers, drained
6 anchovy fillets, drained
1 clove garlic, crushed
1tbsp mustard powder
Pinch each: ground cloves, ground ginger and freshly grated nutmeg
Pepper

1. Place olives in food processor. Set motor running and gradually pour in oil. Switch off motor. Add remaining ingredients.

2. Process to a smooth paste. Cover and refrigerate. Serve on mini Melba toast or fill mini tartlets.

Note: If an electric blender is used, combine oil, lemon juice and brandy before remaining ingredients. Some machines may require additional oil.

Tapenade freezes well.

Red Caviar Dip
Makes approximately 425ml (³/₄pt)

225g (8oz) cottage cheese
1 carton natural yoghourt (142ml/5fl oz)
1tbsp parsley, finely chopped
2tbsp lemon juice
Salt
Pepper
75g (3oz) red caviar

1. Blend together all ingredients except the caviar.
2. Reserve 1tsp caviar for decoration. Fold remainder into cottage cheese mixture.
3. Mound dip in glass dish. Sprinkle with remaining caviar. Refrigerate and serve chilled.

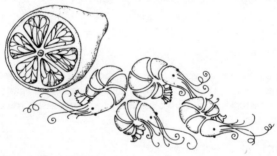

Shrimp or Prawn Dip
Makes approximately 1.25 litres (2pt)

450g (1lb) prawns or shrimps, boiled and peeled
2 cartons sour cream (142ml/5fl oz each)
175g (6oz) cream cheese
2tbsp lemon juice
1tsp Worcestershire sauce
½tsp curry powder
8 black olives, pitted
2tbsp dry sherry

Combine all the ingredients together and process or blend for 1 minute. Serve chilled with courgette strips.

5. Appetisers and Hors-d'oeuvres

What's the difference between appetisers and hors-d'oeuvres? You may well ask. Much depends upon which side of the Atlantic you happen to be. However, many of the recipes in this section do make interesting party nibbles as well as excellent dinner party starters. All are light, nourishing and relatively non-fattening. Few involve elaborate cookery and most may be altered or adjusted to suit your occasion.

On the other hand breaded lamb chops, sauced chicken joints, or fried frogs' legs are not included, for several reasons: they are impossible to eat standing up with any degree of elegance; they're fattening; and they belong on a buffet supper table. So forget the caterers' current craze.

Let's start with eggs.

Eggs

Hard-boiled, stuffed, or otherwise, eggs make good sense on the cocktail party scene. They're versatile, inexpensive and quick to organise. The best way to hard boil eggs is to cover them with cold water in a saucepan. Bring to a rolling boil. Turn off heat but leave pan on stove for at least 10 minutes. Cool eggs under running water and shell.

China Tea Eggs
Makes 24 halves

12 eggs, hard-boiled
142ml (¼pt) soy sauce
25g (1oz) China tea leaves
2tsp cinnamon
750ml (1½pt) water
Salt

1. Crack egg shells but do not peel.
2. In a saucepan bring soy sauce, tea leaves, cinnamon, salt and water to boil. Cover and simmer for 10 minutes.
3. Add eggs to pan. Cover and continue to simmer for 1 hour

29

(eggs must be covered by liquid).

4. Cool eggs in liquid. Shell just before the party. Split in half. Serve nestling on a bed of lettuce leaves.

Black Velvet Eggs
Makes almost 575ml (1pt); serves 6 as a starter

Lovely mimosa-yellow mixture surrounded by black caviar. It takes all of 10 seconds to prepare with a food processor.

8 eggs, hard-boiled, peeled and quartered
Salt
Pepper
275ml (½pt) mayonnaise, made with 2 egg yolks, 275ml (½pt) oil and ½tbsp vinegar
100g (4oz) jar black lumpfish caviar

1. Process eggs with salt and pepper.
2. Add mayonnaise slowly.
3. Mound mixture in a dish and chill.
4. Surround with black caviar. Serve very cold with small biscuits and cucumber sticks.

Note: Taste is the governing factor here. You might like more or less mayonnaise mixed with the eggs. Friends voted this particular combination best.

Stuffed Egg Platter

An assortment of stuffed eggs provides scope for your imagination and most people's predilection. Here are four stuffings to try.

Devilled Egg Baskets
Makes 12 halves

6 eggs, hard-boiled and peeled
1tsp anchovy paste
50g (2oz) prawns, chopped
1tsp Worcestershire sauce
1tbsp mayonnaise
Salt and pepper
6 green pepper rings cut in half for decoration

1. Split eggs. Remove yolks, set aside whites.
2. Pound yolks. Blend or process with anchovy paste, prawns, Worcestershire sauce and mayonnaise. Season.
3. Spoon mixture into egg whites. Insert green pepper ends into egg whites to resemble basket handles.

Salmon Stuffed Eggs
Makes 12 halves

6 eggs, hard-boiled and peeled
100g (4oz) fresh salmon, cooked and flaked
2tbsp mayonnaise
2tbsp lemon juice
ltsp horseradish sauce
Salt
Pepper
Black olives for decoration

1. Split eggs. Remove yolks and set whites aside.
2. Blend, pound or process yolks with remaining ingredients.
3. Mound filling into whites. Top with a triangular shape of black olive.

Note: No fresh salmon? Use the canned variety. No salmon? Substitute tunafish.

Ham and Pineapple Stuffed Eggs
Makes 12 halves

6 eggs, hard-boiled and peeled
100g (4oz) ham, minced
25g (1oz) gherkins, finely chopped
75g (3oz) pineapple, crushed and drained
2tbsp mayonnaise
ltsp Dijon made mustard
Salt
Pepper
Parsley for decoration, finely chopped

1. Split eggs. Remove yolks and save the whites.
2. Sieve yolks and mix with remaining ingredients. Use food processor if available.
3. Mound mixture into egg white halves. Sprinkle with parsley.

31

Eggs with Red Caviar
Makes 12 halves

6 eggs, hard-boiled and peeled
50g (2oz) cream cheese
1tbsp sour cream
2tbsp chives, minced
2tbsp lemon juice
2tbsp red 'caviar'
Salt
Pepper

1. Cut eggs in half. Remove yolks and save whites.
2. Sieve, pound or process yolks. Blend with cream cheese, sour cream, chives, lemon juice and seasoning. Fold in the caviar.
3. Pipe filling into egg whites. Top with caviar. Serve chilled.

Apple and Liver Bites
Makes approximately 60

6 small eating apples (Cox's are best)
100g (4oz) butter
225g (8oz) chicken livers
9 slices white bread

1. Stamp out rounds 40mm (1½in) diameter from bread slices using a pastry cutter or coffee cup. Toast rounds or make oven croûtons (see p14).
2. Core apples and slice in rings approximately 6mm (¼in) thick. Sauté in butter until almost tender. Drain on kitchen paper.
3. Season and sauté chicken livers. Drain.
4. Place an apple ring on each slice of toast or croûton. Top with chicken liver. Secure with a cocktail pick. Serve warm.

Almond Olive Balls
Makes 30

Make ahead of time and refrigerate.

200g (7oz) jar pimento-stuffed olives
75g (3oz) cream cheese
175g (6oz) almonds, blanched, toasted and chopped

1. Drain and dry olives.
2. Beat cream cheese. Mound around each olive.
3. Roll olive balls in chopped almonds.
4. Serve in petit four paper cases, chilled.

Celery Logs
Makes approximately 36

I first made celery logs at school with blue cheese but the capers in this American recipe give an old idea a new taste.

1 head of celery, cleaned, scraped
100g (4oz) cream cheese
2tbsp sour cream
25g (1oz) butter
2tbsp capers, minced
1tbsp paprika
½tsp mixed mustard
1tbsp green pepper, minced
Salt

1. Mix last 8 ingredients together.
2. Fill each celery rib with mixture and chill.
3. Slice ribs into 25mm (1in) logs and serve with rock salt.

Fish in Rum
Serves approximately 24

The fish in this recipe 'cooks' in the fridge, but don't tell your friends until after the party.

450g (1lb) fresh haddock
2tsp salt
142ml (¼pt) water
4tbsp lemon juice
142ml (¼pt) white rum
Black pepper

1. Skin and cube the fish. Soak in salted water for 2 hours.
2. Drain fish. Rinse in fresh water. Place in glass dish and cover with lemon juice and rum. Seal with cling film. Chill overnight in fridge.
3. Sprinkle with freshly ground black pepper. Serve with picks on the side for guests to help themselves.

Smoked Salmon Pâté
Makes approximately 275g (10oz)

The aspic may sound a fiddle, but it provides this pâté with a wonderfully smooth, velvety texture.

225g (8oz) smoked salmon pieces
2tsp lemon juice
½tsp paprika
142ml (¼pt) single cream
1tsp aspic powder, 6 tbsp water
Red 'caviar'

1. Skin and bone fish. Cut into small pieces.
2. Blend or process fish with lemon juice, paprika and cream until smooth.
3. Mix aspic powder with water according to instructions on the packet. Place in fridge to 'set' for 10 minutes.
4. Whisk the almost set aspic into fish mixture until well blended. Pour into a 450g (1lb) dish and set in fridge.
5. Serve on croûtons, biscuits, or rounds of brown bread and butter. Top with specks of red 'caviar'.

Note: This pâté can be frozen. Thaw overnight in fridge or for 3 hours at room temperature.

Mussels in Mayonnaise
Makes approximately 50

900g (2lb) mussels
1 onion, roughly chopped
275ml (½pt) dry white wine
4tbsp parsley, finely chopped
275ml (½pt) stiff mayonnaise
½tsp paprika

1. Wash, clean and de-beard mussels. Place in a pan with onion, wine, and 1tbsp parsley. Cook over a high heat for 5–6 minutes.
2. Remove mussels from their shells. Reserve shells and roughly chop mussel flesh. (Any mussel which has not opened during cooking must be discarded.)
3. Mix cooled chopped mussels with 2tbsp parsley. Fold into stiff mayonnaise. Spoon filling into mussel shells. Sprinkle with parsley and a dash of paprika.

Note: This recipe works best if you make the mayonnaise with lemon juice instead of vinegar.

Scallops and Bacon
Makes 32

An alternative for those who hate oysters but like the idea of 'angels on horseback'.

16 scallops, prepared
Salt
Pepper
Lemon juice
16 rashers streaky bacon
Tartar sauce

1. Sprinkle scallops with salt, pepper and lemon juice. Cut in half.
2. Derind bacon. Divide each slice in half and wrap one half round each half scallop. Secure with cocktail stick.
3. Grill under a moderate heat for approximately 5 minutes each side.
4. Serve with tartar sauce, mounded on tiny squares of toast.

Note: Very good tartar sauce can be obtained from your local shops. If you want to make your own just add 2tsp each chopped capers, chopped gherkins and chopped parsley, and 1tsp each lemon juice and chopped chives, to 142ml (¼pt) mayonnaise.

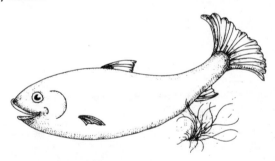

Salmon Cured with Dill
Serves approximately 24

Fresh dill is not easy to find in the shops, so growing your own might be the answer. It's delicious with all fish.

450g (1lb) fresh salmon
2tbsp black peppercorns
2tbsp white peppercorns
2tbsp coarse salt crystals
2tbsp sugar
3 large sprigs of fresh dill

1. Grind together the peppercorns, sugar and salt.
2. Slit open the salmon. Thoroughly rub the curing mixture all over the fish.
3. Place one sprig of dill in the bottom of the dish, one sprig inside the fish, last sprig on top of the fish. Cover with strong cling film and foil. Place a heavy weight on top. Refrigerate for 3 days. Turn fish daily. There will be a little more liquid in the dish each day as it is forced out of the salmon. Do not remove the juices.
4. Extract fish from marinade mixture. Scrape away every scrap of peppery liquid. Discard the dill. Pat fish dry and cut in thin slices.
5. Serve salmon either on picks or spread over buttered pumpernickel.

Avocado Spread
Makes just under 275ml ($^{1}/_{2}$pt)

2 ripe avocados
100g (4oz) cottage cheese
2tbsp lemon juice
$^{1}/_{2}$tsp chopped parsley
Salt
Pepper
$^{1}/_{4}$tsp Worcestershire sauce
5 or 6 walnuts, chopped

1. Peel avocados. Mash the pulp with cottage cheese and lemon juice.
2. Add parsley and season well. Add Worcestershire sauce to taste.
3. Fold chopped walnuts into mixture. Serve on small crackers or rye bread.

Note: Add a drop of green colouring to improve colour if required.

Aubergine Spread
Makes approximately 575ml (1pt)

Served with hunks of Polish black bread, this makes a substantial snack best suited to an outdoor event.

4tbsp oil
1 onion, chopped
2 cloves garlic, sliced
2 large aubergines, unpeeled, cut in cubes
2 green peppers, deseeded and sliced

36

4 medium carrots, sliced
425g (15oz) can tomato pulp
75g (3oz) can tomato paste
Salt
Pepper

1. Heat oil. Sauté onion and garlic.
2. Add green pepper, carrot and seasonings. Continue cooking until golden brown. Add more oil if necessary. Watch and stir often.
3. Add a little water to prevent vegetables sticking to pan. Stir in aubergines. Cover. Cook over low heat for 1½ hours. Stir frequently.
4. When vegetables are soft, uncover and reduce any accumulated liquid over high heat.
5. Add tomato pulp and paste. Cook for a further 10 minutes.
6. Beat mixture until smooth. Cool and refrigerate.

Easy Smooth Liver Pâté
Makes approximately 450g (1lb) pâté, sufficient for 32 canapés

225g (8oz) lamb's liver, sliced
225g (8oz) chicken livers, sliced
100g (4oz) streaky bacon, sliced
1tsp mustard powder
1 onion, finely chopped
1 clove garlic, crushed
Salt
Pepper
50g (2oz) lard, melted
1 egg

1. Blend or process all ingredients together until quite smooth.
2. Turn into an oiled 450g (1lb) loaf tin. Cover with grease-proof paper, and then foil.
3. Stand prepared loaf tin in a roasting pan half filled with water. Cook in a pre-heated oven, 150°C (300°F) Gas 2, for 2 hours. Cool. Serve piled on mini-toasts and topped with specks of red pepper, tomato or halved stuffed olives.

Stuffed Baby Beets
Makes 24

400g (14oz) can new whole baby beetroots
100g (4oz) cream cheese, softened
2tbsp gherkins, finely chopped
2tsp chives, finely chopped
1tbsp lemon juice

1. Drain beetroots and pat dry. Slice each beet in half and
   hollow out centre with a melon scoop.
2. Mix remaining ingredients together; stuff into beets.
3. Chill. Serve on a bed of fresh green lettuce.

Devilled Prunes
Makes 24

24 large prunes
575ml (1pt) cold tea
275ml (½pt) water
4 rashers streaky bacon, derinded and finely chopped
142ml (¼pt) double cream
1tbsp Worcestershire sauce
50g (1oz) butter

1. Soak prunes overnight in tea and water.
2. Drain. Dry, cut through one side and remove stone.
3. Fry bacon in butter until crisp.
4. Whip cream until stiff. Fold in Worcestershire sauce.
5. Stuff a little bacon into each prune. Finish with cream piped
   along the top. Chill.

Marinated Mushrooms
Makes approximately 30

450g (1lb) fresh small mushroom caps, wiped clean
3 spring onions, chopped (white part only)
275ml (½pt) each red wine vinegar and oil
1tbsp tarragon, chopped
2 cloves garlic, crushed
Salt and pepper

1. Place mushrooms and onions in a china dish.
2. Mix together remaining ingredients. Pour over mushroom
   and onion mixture.
3. Cover with cling film and refrigerate for 24 hours. Stir
   twice.
4. Drain mushrooms. Wipe off onion. Serve on picks.

Red Pepper Spirals
Makes 32

4 large red peppers
3tbsp parsley, chopped
2tbsp hazelnuts, chopped
3tbsp oil
½ clove garlic, crushed
Salt
Pepper

1. Toast and char peppers. While still hot, slice each pepper into eighths lengthwise. Remove fleshy stem part, seeds and skin.
2. Blend, pound or process parsley, nuts, oil and garlic together to a fine purée. Check and adjust seasoning.
3. Spread a thin layer of purée on each pepper strip.
4. Roll up each strip. Start from the narrow end. Secure with a pick.
5. Arrange spirals on a glass dish with shiny black oil-cured olives.

Note: Buy this type of black olive loose from a delicatessen.
   Replace parsley with fresh basil if you have some in the garden for even better results.

Salmon and Walnut Bomb
Makes approximately 425ml (³/₄pt)

100g (4oz) canned salmon, drained, boned and flaked
225g (8oz) cottage cheese
1tbsp gherkin, chopped
1tbsp lemon juice
50g (2oz) walnuts, finely chopped
4tbsp parsley, finely chopped
Salt
Pepper

1. Whip cottage cheese until creamy. Mix with salmon, lemon juice, gherkin and seasonings. Chill overnight in fridge.

2. Mix parsley with walnuts.
3. Form salmon mixture into large bomb shape and roll in walnut mixture. Chill for at least 2 hours before serving.
4. Serve surrounded with small crackers and mini toasts. Provide implements for spreading.

Note: If preferred, you can make lots of little salmon balls. Roll in nut and herb mixture. Serve chilled in petit four paper cases.

Stuffed Mushrooms (1)
Makes 24

Medium-sized mushroom caps stuffed with interesting mixtures make ideal party nibbles. Prepare ahead of time and warm when required.

24 fresh mushrooms
150g (5oz) butter
2tbsp lemon juice
2tbsp shallots, finely chopped
1 clove garlic, crushed
100g (4oz) breadcrumbs
1 egg, beaten
2tbsp dry vermouth
1tbsp parsley, chopped
24 anchovy fillets, rolled

1. Wipe mushrooms and remove stalks. Melt butter in a heavy pan and sauté mushroom caps briefly. Sprinkle with lemon juice. Set aside.
2. Mince mushroom stalks. Sauté in remaining butter with shallots and garlic. Stir in egg, breadcrumbs, vermouth and parsley. Cook for a few minutes.
3. Stuff mushrooms with mixture. Dot with butter. Grill for 5 minutes. Top with tightly rolled anchovy fillets.

Stuffed Mushrooms (2)
Makes 24

24 mushrooms
150g (5oz) butter
2tbsp dry white wine
25g (1oz) smoked ham, finely chopped
½tsp oregano
25g (1oz) Parmesan cheese, grated
25g (1oz) Gruyère cheese, grated
2 eggs, hard-boiled and finely chopped
3tbsp parsley, chopped

Salt and pepper

1. Remove stalks from mushroom caps. Chop stalks and sauté in butter. Add ham and wine. Cook for a few minutes. Add remaining ingredients. Mix well.
2. Fill mushroom caps. Dot with butter.
3. Bake on a greased tray in a pre-heated oven, 200°C (400°F) Gas 6, for 10 minutes.

Scandinavian Prawns
Serves approximately 36

1kg (2.2lb) fresh prawns, boiled, shelled and deveined

Marinade
1tbsp each ready-mixed mustard and sugar
2tbsp wine vinegar
1tsp lemon juice, 125ml (4fl oz) oil
1tbsp parsley, finely chopped

1. Combine marinade ingredients in a bottle and shake well.
2. Toss prawns in marinade. Cover and chill for a few hours.
3. Drain prawns. Serve on picks.

Classic Taramasalata
Makes approximately 550ml (1pt)

2 slices white bread, crusts removed
225g (8oz) smoked cod's roe, skinned
3tbsp lemon juice
1 clove garlic, crushed
275ml (½pt) oil

1. Wet the bread and squeeze out. It should be moist.
2. blend or process cod's roe, lemon juice and garlic.
3. Continue to process and gradually add oil. Mixture should take on the consistency of mayonnaise.
4. Serve with oatcakes, crackers and radishes.

Quick Cook's Taramasalata
Makes approximately 425ml (¾pt)

175g (6oz) jar cod's roe
175g (6oz) cream cheese
Lemon juice

1 clove garlic, crushed
ltsp oil

Process all the ingredients together. It's delicious. Pile on crackers or French bread canapé bases.

Note: Obtain cod's roe from a delicatessen.

Smoked Trout Brandade
Makes 275ml (½pt)
1 pink smoked trout
50g (2oz) cream cheese
25g (1oz) butter, melted
Salt
Pepper
2tbsp lemon juice
2 heads Belgium endive

1. Skin and bone out fish.
2. Process all ingredients, except endive, and reduce to a purée.
3. Pile mixture into a 275ml (½pt) dish and chill.
4. Remove from fridge 1 hour before required. Use to stuff endive leaves.

Note: This recipe is also good served as a dip. Add a little cream if purée is too stiff.

Steak Tartar
Makes approximately 225g (8oz); will cover 24 small canapés

225g (8oz) raw beef, freshly minced
2tbsp onion, finely chopped
2tsp Worcestershire sauce
Salt and pepper

1. Mix all ingredients together.
2. Use to top canapé bases, or mound and serve surrounded with salty biscuits or crudités for guests to help themselves. Decorate with capers and tiny cubes of onion.

Tapas

Every bar in Spain sports a selection of these pre-dinner snacks. Originally simple slices of bread placed over sherry glasses to keep out the flies, they're now almost a meal in themselves, often rather moist. Spaniards serve tapas on small plates with tiny forks. If you plan a Spanish evening at least provide plenty of picks and a big pile of napkins – maybe even make it an outdoor occasion. Make a selection of the following for fun.

Clams with Olives
Makes 12

100g (4oz) canned clams, drained
2tsp white wine vinegar
½ onion, finely chopped
½tsp Tabasco sauce
10 black olives, pitted

Mix clam juice with wine vinegar, onion and Tabasco sauce. Pour over clams. Garnish with olives.

Artichokes with Herb Sauce
Makes 9–10

225g (8oz) canned artichoke hearts, drained
6tbsp olive oil
2tbsp lemon juice
2tsp mixed fresh herbs, finely chopped (eg dill, marjoram, thyme, parsley)

1. Blend together the oil, lemon juice and herbs.
2. Pour dressing over the artichoke hearts.

Squid in Tomato Sauce
Serves 12

Stuffed squid are called *Calamares rellenos* in Spain.

100g (4oz) canned squid
142ml (¼pt) tomato juice
1tbsp sherry
½ clove garlic, crushed
½tsp Tabasco sauce

1. Drain squid and chop into slices 6mm (¼in) thick.
2. Combine other ingredients.
3. Spoon sauce over squid.

Grilled Prawns
Makes 12

12 large fresh prawns, cleaned
2tbsp oil
2 cloves garlic, crushed
¼tsp rock salt

1. Mix together oil, garlic and salt.
2. Brush prawns with mixture.
3. Grill under a high heat for 5 minutes.

Note: Very good on a barbeque.

Mussels in Spicy Sauce
Makes 12

225g (8oz) fresh mussels, steamed in white wine
2tbsp mayonnaise
2tsp prepared mustard
1tsp white wine
½tsp lemon juice
1 red pepper, sliced in short strips

1. Shell mussels and place them in a serving dish. Mix together the remaining ingredients.
2. Spoon sauce over the mussels.

Note: This recipe does *not* taste as good made with canned or bottled mussels.

Yoghourt Cheese with Walnuts
Makes 275ml (½pt)

2 cartons natural yoghourt (142ml/5fl oz each)
100g (4oz) walnuts, chopped
1tsp onion, minced
Salt
Pepper
6 black olives, pitted and sliced

1. Line a colander with a double layer of cheese cloth. Allow sufficient cloth over the edge to fold back over the surface of the yoghourt.
2. Place yoghourt in colander. Cover with excess cloth. Stand colander in a container. Drain and refrigerate overnight.
3. When required, add onions, walnuts and seasoning. Mound mixture in a pretty dish and decorate with olive slices. Serve with warm pitta bread.

6. Hot Nibbles, Bakes and Fritters

Warm nibbles on a cold night are always welcome, and they are easy to organise with a little help from your oven, hot tray or hostess trolley. Here are a few tips to help:

Make pastry cases in advance, bake 'blind' and freeze. Remember, tartlets, barquettes, etc, must come to room temperature before filling.

Filled quiches or pizzas simply need reheating.

Cook, fill and freeze mini choux buns weeks ahead of time. For perfectionists who insist choux paste be crisp, freeze buns unfilled, then crisp, cool and fill 2 hours before the party. Ordinary mortals have insufficient time to consider anything so complicated. For us the importance lies in *remembering* to extract the completed choux from the freezer in time to defrost thoroughly.

Swedish meat balls and cheese mouthfuls provide further ammunition for a cook-ahead campaign. Deep fry both in advance. Freeze. On the party day, set on a baking tray and warm through.

Fritters present more of a problem, so save them for when you employ staff. The exception might be a teenage offspring in need of funds and practice for Cookery 'A' level. (You'll also need a deep-fat fryer.)

Note: To bake 'blind', line a tart tin or large flan dish, 20cm (8in) in diameter, with pastry. Prick the base. Cover with greaseproof paper, weighed down with a few dried beans or pasta. Bake in centre of oven for 15 minutes at 200°C (400°F) Gas 6 until pastry is set. Remove beans and paper. Reduce heat to 180°C (350°F) Gas 4 and bake for a further 5-10 minutes. For mini tartlets, barquettes, etc, simply place an unfilled mould on top. Be sure to thoroughly prick bases.

Barquettes
Makes 10–12

Pastry boats filled to suit your mood and pocket. Success depends upon rolling out the rich pastry very thinly – less than 3mm (⅛in) thick.

100g (4oz) flour
Salt
50g (2oz) butter
50g (2oz) Cheddar cheese, finely grated
1 egg, beaten

1. Sift together the flour and salt. Add butter. Bring to breadcrumb stage. Mix in the cheese.
2. Add egg and stir until ingredients stick together. Knead lightly to smooth dough.
3. Roll out pastry. Line pastry boats. Thoroughly prick the base of barquettes. Set a second mould on pastry to prevent pastry puffing up.
4. Bake 'blind' in a pre-heated oven, 200°C (400°F) Gas 6, for 7–8 minutes. Remove empty mould. Prick bottom of boats again and return to oven for 3 minutes until shells just begin to colour.
5. Cool on wire rack. Stack carefully in rigid containers. Freeze.
6. Thaw and fill when required.

Ideas for filling barquettes:

Any flavoured cream cheese (see pp15–16). Use a toning decoration.

Lemon-flavoured butter topped with red or black caviar. Decorate with chopped egg or twist of lemon. A fine rim of piping around the edge of the boat looks fun if you have time to spare.

White crab meat mixed with mayonnaise. Top with a speck of red pimento.

Flaked fish – haddock or salmon mixed with chopped hard-boiled eggs in a béchamel sauce.

Baby Quiches
Makes 36

75g (3oz) butter
75g (3oz) lard

325g (12oz) flour
A pinch of salt
3tbsp water

Egg mixture:

6 eggs
142ml (½pt) milk
Salt
Pepper

1. Rub butter and lard into flour and salt. Add water and mix to a stiff dough.
2. Roll out the dough and cut into 36 circles, diameter 7.5cm (3in). Fit pastry circles into patty tins.
3. Spoon in chosen filling (see below).
4. Whisk together egg, milk and seasonings. Pour mixture into filled tartlets.
5. Bake for 25 minutes in a pre-heated oven, 180°C (350°F) Gas 4.

Ideas for fillings (quantities given are each sufficient for 12 baby quiches):

Spinach and cottage cheese
100g (4oz) cottage cheese
100g (4oz) chopped spinach, thawed
Divide cottage cheese between tartlets. Add spinach. Top with egg mixture.

Tuna and olives
One 99g (3½oz) can tuna, drained and flaked
12 stuffed olives, sliced
Place fish in bottom of tartlets. Top with olives, then egg mixture.

Prawn and mushroom
100g (4oz) peeled prawns, chopped
50g (2oz) mushrooms, sliced
12 tiny squares green pepper
Divide mushrooms and prawns between tartlets. Top with egg mixture. Decorate each one with central speck of green pepper.

Ham and onion
100g (4oz) cooked ham
1 medium onion
12 small sprigs parsley
Mince or process ham and onion together. Pile into tartlets. Top with egg mixture and decorate each tartlet with parsley.

Courgette and cheese
100g (4oz) small courgettes, thinly sliced
50g (2oz) mature Cheddar cheese, grated
Blanch courgettes for one minute only. Arrange in tartlets with cheese. Top with egg mixture.

Liver and bacon
4 rashers streaky bacon, derinded and chopped
100g (4oz) chicken livers, chopped
25g (1oz) butter
Sauté chicken livers and bacon together in a little butter for 6–7 minutes. Divide between tartlets. Top each one with egg mixture.

Filled Pastry Fingers
Makes 72

175g (6oz) lard
175g (6oz) butter
900g (2lb) flour
Salt
2tbsp water
1 egg, beaten

1. Rub fats into flour and salt until the mixture resembles breadcrumbs.
2. Add water and mix to a stiff dough. Divide dough into 6 portions.
3. Roll out 1 portion to fit Swiss roll tin.
4. Spread with filling (see below).
5. Roll out another portion of dough to fit tin. Place on top of filling, damp edges and seal.
6. Mark pastry into 24 fingers. Glaze with beaten egg and sprinkle with salt. Cook for 20 minutes in a pre-heated oven, 200°C (400°F) Gas 6. Turn on to wire tray. Cool and slice.
7. Repeat with remaining 4 portions.

Finger Fillings
Each sufficient for 24 fingers

Gentleman's delight: 25g (1oz) softened butter mixed with 1tsp Gentleman's Relish.

Mango curry: 1tbsp curry paste mixed with 1tbsp mango chutney.

Peanut spread: 2tbsp peanut butter mixed with 25g (1oz) chopped peanuts.

Hot tomato: 2tbsp tomato purée, a dash of Tabasco sauce and 2tsp Worcestershire sauce.

Marmite special: 25g (1oz) cream cheese mixed with 2tsp Marmite.

Note: These fingers freeze well and are worth making in a big batch. Thaw when required at room temperature for ½ hour, or reheat in the oven, 180°C (350°F) Gas 4, for 15 minutes.

Beignets
Makes approximately 24

Cheese choux paste puffs deep-fried, frozen and reheated in the oven when required. For extra interest wrap choux paste round a single prawn.

Choux paste (p50)
Oil for frying
100g (4oz) Parmesan cheese, grated

1. Prepare the choux paste. Heat the oil to a temperature of 195°C (380°F).
2. Drop teaspoonfuls of mixture into oil and fry for about 7 minutes until golden and puffed.
3. Lift from fat with slotted spoon. Drain on kitchen paper.
4. Roll in Parmesan cheese while still warm. Cool and freeze.
5. Heat on a baking tray in a warm oven when required.

Cheese Mouthfuls
Makes 60

Economical and easy, these freeze beautifully. Just heat and serve on 'the day'.

225g (8oz) old potatoes, peeled and boiled
100g (4oz) each plain flour, softened butter
75g (3oz) Gruyère cheese, grated
1 small egg, beaten
Pinch each nutmeg, paprika, salt

1. Mash potatoes. Beat together well all other ingredients and add to the potatoes. You may not need all the egg.
2. Taste and add more salt if necessary.
3. With a small teaspoon drop blobs of the mixture 5cm (2in) apart on to a lightly buttered baking sheet.
4. Cook in a pre-heated oven, 220°C (425°F) Gas 7, for 15 minutes. Serve warm.

Cheese Choux Paste
Makes approximately 24

142ml (¼pt) water
40g (1½oz) butter
100g (4oz) flour
2 eggs
50g (2oz) Cheddar or Gruyère cheese, grated
Salt
Pepper

1. Melt butter in water. Bring to boil. Remove from heat.
2. Tip in flour all at once. Beat until smooth. Return to heat and cook, stirring until mixture leaves the side of the pan.
3. Beat in eggs one at a time. Use a food processor if you have one.
4. Stir in cheese and season.
5. Drop spoonfuls on a baking sheet and cook at 200°C (400°F) Gas 6 for 25 minutes.
6. Cool on wire rack. Fill with any cream cheese filling (see pp15–16) or sharp mornay sauce (2tbsp butter, 2tbsp flour, 275ml (½pt) milk, mustard and cayenne pepper).

Cheese Straws
Makes 40

100g (4oz) flour
Salt
Cayenne pepper
50g (2oz) butter
50g (2oz) tasty Cheddar cheese
1 egg yolk
Cold water
Paprika

1. Season flour with salt and cayenne pepper. Rub in butter. Bring mixture to texture of breadcrumbs. Add cheese.

50

2. Stir in egg yolk and sufficient cold water to form a stiff dough.
3. Roll out paste. Cut into straws approximately 76mm (3in) long and 6mm (¼in) wide.
4. Bake in a pre-heated oven, 200°C (400°F) Gas 6, for 10–15 minutes.
5. Cool on wire rack. Dust with paprika before serving.

Savoury Cheesecake
Makes 30–32 small squares

100g (4oz) cheese biscuits or crackers
50g (2oz) butter, melted
75g (3oz) butter, cubed
Salt
Pepper
Celery salt
Paprika
5tbsp single cream
2 eggs, separated
350g (12oz) Cheddar cheese, grated
100g (4oz) salted peanuts, chopped
Cucumber sticks
Watercress

1. Crush biscuits and mix with melted butter. Press into a 20cm (8in) square tin.
2. Cream together remaining butter, seasonings to taste, cream and egg yolks.
3. Add the cheese and peanuts.
4. Whisk egg whites until stiff. Fold into butter/cream mixture and pile into prepared tin.
5. Cook in a pre-heated oven, 150°C (300°F) Gas 2, for 1 hour. When cold cut into small squares. Garnish with cucumber sticks and watercress.

Gorgonzola Bites
Makes 40

50g (2oz) butter
175g (6oz) Gorgonzola cheese
225g (8oz) flour
1 egg, beaten
Salt
Pepper

1. Cream butter until soft. Mash cheese and add to butter. Add egg and seasonings.

2. Blend flour into butter/cheese mixture.
3. Knead to a smooth dough. Add a little water if too dry. Chill for 30 minutes.
4. Roll dough out into a rectangle. Cut into 2.5cm (1in) squares. Cook on a baking sheet in a pre-heated oven, 220°C (425°F) Gas 7, for 12–15 minutes.

Cream and Leek Flan
Makes approximately 24 small slices

1×20cm (8in) pastry case, baked 'blind'
900g (2lb) leeks, thoroughly cleaned
25g (1oz) butter
Pinch of nutmeg
100g (4oz) ham, diced
3 egg yolks
275ml (½pt) double cream
Salt
Pepper

1. Chop white part of leeks and discard the green tops.
2. Melt butter in heavy pan. Add leeks and soften over a low heat.
3. Add ham and continue cooking for 2 minutes, then spread mixture over base of pastry case.
4. Beat together eggs and cream. Add seasonings. Pour over leek and ham mixture.
5. Dot with butter. Bake in a pre-heated oven, 190°C (375°F) Gas 5, for approximately 35 minutes. When cold, cut into neat triangles.
6. Serve warm when required.

Fried Cheese Balls
Makes approximately 30

175g (6oz) tasty Cheddar cheese, grated
1tbsp flour

Salt
Pepper
3 egg whites, beaten
Parmesan cheese, grated

1. Blend together the flour and seasonings. Add Cheddar cheese.
2. Fold in egg whites. Shape into balls approximately 25mm (1in) in diameter.
3. Roll each ball in Parmesan cheese.
4. Deep-fry until golden brown. Drain on kitchen paper. Serve warm with picks.

Note: Cook ahead of time. Freeze. Defrost and crisp in warm oven when required.

Lobster Balls
Makes approximately 30

275g (10oz) creamed potatoes
50g (2oz) lobster paste
2 eggs
Breadcrumbs
Oil for frying

1. Blend together potatoes and lobster paste. Add one egg. Mix well and shape into balls, approximately the size of a walnut.
2. Egg and breadcrumb the balls. Deep fry for a few minutes. Drain on kitchen paper.

Note: These may be reheated in a warm oven if prepared in advance.

Clam fritters
Makes 36

175g (6oz) flour
175g (6oz) butter, softened
Salt
3 eggs, separated
340ml (12fl oz) light ale
100g (4oz) canned clams, drained
1tbsp parsley, finely chopped
1tbsp chives, snipped
2tbsp oil

1. Sift together the flour and salt. Add 50g (2oz) butter. Process for a few seconds.

2. Beat egg yolks and add to flour and butter mixture.
3. Run machine and gradually add beer. When mixed, allow to stand in a warm place for 1 hour.
4. Stir clams and herbs into batter.
5. Fold stiffly beaten egg whites into batter mixture.
6. In a heavy pan heat together remaining butter with oil. When very hot, drop in scant tablespoonfuls of batter. Brown fritters on both sides.
7. Drain and serve hot with plenty of paper napkins to mop up excess moisture.

Note: Vongole – tiny clams – are available from most up-market food stores.

Cauliflower Fritters
Serves 20

Unusual because the batter is made with tomato juice instead of milk.

1 large cauliflower, divided into small sprigs
Salt
Pepper
100g (4oz) flour
2 eggs, separated
275ml (½pt) tomato juice
Oil for frying

1. Lightly cook the cauliflower sprigs in boiling salted water until just tender. Refresh under cold water. Pat dry.
2. Make up a batter with tomato juice, flour and egg yolks. Season.
3. Whisk egg whites and fold into batter.
4. Dip cauliflower sprigs into tomato batter. Deep fry in hot oil for 1–2 minutes. Drain on kitchen paper.

Brussels Sprouts in Yoghourt Batter
Makes approximately 40

900g (2lb) baby Brussels sprouts, washed
Salt
Batter:
100g (4oz) flour
Salt
2 eggs, separated
Two 142ml (½pt) cartons natural yoghourt
Oil for frying

1. Lightly cook Brussels sprouts in boiling salted water.

2. Blend or process together flour, salt, egg yolks and yoghourt, to make a smooth batter.
3. Whisk egg whites until stiff. Fold into batter.
4. Dip sprouts in batter. Deep fry for 2–3 minutes. Drain, and serve hot.

French Fried Fennel
Serves approximately 36

2 large fennel roots, sliced
100g (4oz) flour
2 eggs
275ml (½pt) milk
Oil for frying

1. Whisk together milk, flour and eggs to form a smooth batter.
2. Dip strips of fennel in batter and fry in hot oil for only 2–3 minutes. The fennel must be crisp on the outside and firm inside.
3. Serve with lemon mayonnaise or Shrimp or Prawn Dip (see p28).

Fish Triangles
Makes approximately 36

Rich cream cheese pastry morsels filled with smoked haddock and egg mixture. My family like them even better with sardine and egg filling.

100g (4oz) butter
100g (4oz) cream cheese
100g (4oz) flour
100g (4oz) smoked haddock, poached
Itbsp lemon juice
Itsp curry powder
2 hard-boiled eggs, chopped
Salt
Pepper

1. Blend or process butter and cream cheese. Add flour. Process for a few seconds. Knead dough into a ball and place in fridge to relax.
2. Make fish filling: mix fish with lemon juice, curry powder and eggs. Taste and season.
3. Roll out pastry. Section into 5cm (2in) squares.
4. Place a teaspoonful of filling on each square. Moisten edges with water. Fold pastry to form triangles and pinch together edges. Make a tiny slit in the top of each triangle.

5. Bake in a pre-heated oven, 230°C (450°F) Gas 8, for 10 minutes. Serve warm.

Note: Do not freeze, as the eggs will go rubbery.

Frittata
Cuts into 30 mini squares

A flat omelette served as antipasti in Italy. Make on the morning of the party. It will not freeze.

6 eggs, beaten
50g (2oz) Parmesan cheese, grated
50g (2oz) butter
2tbsp oil
½ onion, finely chopped
Itsp oregano
2tbsp parsley, finely chopped
Salt
Pepper

1. Season eggs. Add cheese, onion and herbs. Beat mixture until thick and frothy.
2. Heat together the butter and oil in a heavy pan. Pour in egg mixture and allow to 'set' for 2 minutes over high heat. Place in a pre-heated oven, 180°C (350°F) Gas 4, for 20–25 minutes.
3. Remove from oven. Allow to cool. Refrigerate.
4. Serve cold, cut into strips on an Italian platter with an assortment of salami, melon cubes, rolls of smoked ham and olives.

Note: Vary ingredients of frittata to suit your inclination. Add 100g (4oz) sliced, blanched courgettes or 100g (4oz) chopped artichoke hearts or your favourite herbs. Occasionally I include diced ham or a few chopped prawns.

French Tomato Tart
Makes 25–30 small slices

1 × 22.5cm (9in) pastry shell, baked 'blind'
3 onions, thinly sliced
2tbsp oil
1kg (2.2lb) fresh ripe tomatoes, skinned, deseeded and chopped
1 clove garlic, crushed
2 tbsp flour
Salt
Pepper

1 carton natural yoghourt (142ml/5fl oz)
1 carton double cream (142ml/5fl oz)
1tbsp tomato purée
1tsp fresh basil, chopped
2 egg whites, beaten

1. Heat oil and sweat onions until soft.
2. Add tomatoes and cook briskly, uncovered, to allow juice to evaporate (this takes about 15 minutes).
3. Add garlic. Sprinkle in flour and stir over heat while mixture thickens. Leave to cool.
4. Beat together yoghourt, cream, tomato purée and seasonings. Add to tomato and onion mixture.
5. Fold in egg whites and basil. Spoon batter into pastry case and bake in pre-heated oven at 190°C (375°F) Gas 5 for 35–40 minutes.
6. Cut in slices and serve warm.

Mini Choux
Makes 24 tiny puffs

35g (1½oz) butter
125ml (¼pt) water
Good pinch of nutmeg
Salt
100g (4oz) flour
2 eggs

1. Melt butter in water with seasonings and bring to rolling boil.
2. Remove pan from heat and tip in all the flour. Beat vigorously.
3. Return pan to heat and continue beating until mixture forms a ball in centre of saucepan. Remove from heat. Beat or process eggs with mixture. Last egg may take a little

time to become absorbed if you are working without a machine.
4. Drop circular mounds of paste on a buttered baking sheet. Cook in a pre-heated oven, 200°C (400°F) Gas 6, for 20 minutes. Choux are cooked when they turn a pale golden colour and have doubled their original size.
5. Remove from oven. Slit each choux with a sharp knife to allow steam to escape. Turn off oven and return puffs for 10 minutes to dry out. Cool completely on a wire rack.
6. Pipe or spoon in chosen filling. Freeze. Bring to room temperature when required.

Suggested fillings:

175g (6oz) cream cheese beaten with 50g (2oz) chopped walnuts.

175g (6oz) cream cheese beaten with 2tbsp red caviar.

175g (6oz) butter beaten with 2tsp anchovy paste.

175g (6oz) Smoked Trout Brandade (see p42).

175g (6oz) smooth home-made pâté.

Note: Use the same recipe, but fill the choux with fresh cream and coat with chocolate, if your friends prefer éclairs with their champagne cocktails.

Spanakopitta (Greek Spinach Pie)
Cuts into 36 small slices

Best made a day ahead.

450g (1lb) frozen spinach, thawed
1 onion, finely chopped
225g (8oz) butter, unsalted
1tsp mint, finely chopped
100g (4oz) Feta cheese, crumbled
50g (2oz) Parmesan cheese, grated
2 eggs, beaten
225g (8oz) phyllo pastry
Salt
Pepper

1. Make the filling first: melt 50g (2oz) butter and sauté onion until soft. Add spinach. Cook mixture for 5 minutes. Set aside to cool.
2. Add Feta and Parmesan cheeses and mint to spinach mixture. Stir well. Fold in eggs. Season.

3. Prepare phyllo pastry case: melt remaining butter. Thoroughly grease a 22.5cm (9in) shallow tart tin. Cover with a leaf of phyllo pastry. Brush with butter. Cover with a further leaf of phyllo pastry. Repeat process until you have a stack of 5 leaves in the tin. (Allow approximately 2.5cm (1in) pastry to overlap edge of tin.)
4. Spread filling over pastry base.
5. Cover filling with 5 more sheets of phyllo pastry. Remember to butter well between each sheet. Tuck top crust down round filling. Roll overlapping crust inwards and tuck around inside edge of pie. Slash top in 2 places. Brush with oil.
6. Bake in pre-heated oven, 180°C (350°F) Gas 4, for 1 hour.
7. Cool. Slice into bite-sized squares when quite cold.

Note: Phyllo pastry can be found in most delicatessens, in the deep-freeze cabinet. It is sold in packs of 400g (14oz). Alternatively, you can make traditional English flaky pastry and bake an Anglo-Greek pie.

Mussel and Mushroom Morsels
Makes approximately 24

Shortcrust pastry:
225g (8oz) flour
150g (5oz) mixture butter and lard

Filling:
125g (4oz) canned mussels, drained
2tbsp ham, finely chopped
2tbsp mushrooms, finely chopped
1 clove garlic, crushed
1tbsp parsley, finely chopped
65g (2½oz) unsalted butter

1. Mix together the ham, mushrooms, garlic, parsley, seasoning and butter to form a paste.
2. Roll out pastry dough into rectangles 3mm (⅛in) thick. Cut into 50mm (2in) squares.
3. Place one mussel and a very small amount of mushroom mixture in the centre of each pastry square. Moisten edges with water. Gather the four corners over filling, pinch and seal them together.
4. Arrange morsels on an ungreased baking sheet. Space them at least 25mm (1in) apart. Prick and brush with beaten egg. Cook in a pre-heated oven, 200°C (400°F) Gas 6, for 15 minutes.

Note: This recipe may be prepared ahead of time and stored in the refrigerator for a few hours until you are ready to bake, just before the party. *Under no circumstances freeze or reheat, because of the mussels.*

Tortillas
Makes 24

A Mexican snack base, it is possible to buy packaged, ready-to-use tortillas in smart grocery shops. However, they are better, and cheaper, if you have time to make your own. They freeze well.

100g (4oz) cornmeal or semolina
100g (4oz) strong white flour
1 egg
1tbsp cold water
Salt

1. Sift together flours and salt. Beat egg with half the water. Mix into dry ingredients.
2. Add remaining water and knead mixture into a firm dough.
3. Divide into 6 pieces. Roll out into rectangles. Divide each into 4.
4. Deep-fry tortillas until crisp and golden. Drain. Serve with Hot Chilli Dip (see p25).

Note: If tortillas have lost their 'bounce' in the freezer, crisp in a hot oven for a few minutes. In any case, they are best served warm.

Mozzarella in Carrozza
Makes 16

An Italian standby, which translated means 'Mozzarella in a carriage', this recipe is delicious and worth considering as a pre-dinner nibble for a few special people – if you have a deep-fat fryer.

8 slices white bread
100g (4oz) Mozzarella cheese, sliced
2 eggs, beaten
2tbsp milk
Salt
Flour
Oil for frying

1. Trim crusts from bread. Divide slices into quarters. Make into 16 mini sandwiches with Mozzarella cheese. Dip edges of bread in cold water and press together to seal.

2. Whisk together egg, milk and a pinch of salt.
3. Dust sandwiches with flour. Dip in beaten egg and milk mixture. Deep-fry in hot oil until golden. Drain on kitchen paper. Serve immediately.

Won Ton Butterflies
Makes approximately 36

Make sure you have a bowl of cold water close to your working surface before starting this recipe.

100g (4oz) Won Ton wrappers (bought from Chinese supermarkets)
225g (8oz) crab meat
50g (2oz) cream cheese
1tsp soy sauce
½tsp Worcestershire sauce
1tbsp lemon juice
Oil for frying

1. Combine crab meat with cream cheese. Add lemon juice, soy sauce and Worcestershire sauce. Mix until well blended.
2. Place 1tsp of filling on one Won Ton square (these are 7.5cm (3in) square). Damp edges and fold over into a triangle.
3. Moisten centre of triangle. With wet fingers and thumbs grasp long ends of dough and bring together. Press down hard so that dough sticks. You now have a butterfly with extended wings.
4. Deep fry until golden. Drain. Serve warm.
5. If prepared in advance reheat on a baking tray in a hot oven, 200°C (400°F) Gas 6, for 5 minutes. Do not cover or butterflies will lose their crisp wings.

Pizzette
Makes 32

450g (1lb) frozen bread dough, thawed and divided in two
Two 400g (14oz) cans tomatoes, drained
1 medium onion, finely sliced
75ml (5tbsp) oil
100g (4oz) Cheddar cheese, grated
Salt and pepper
50g (2oz) canned anchovy fillets
1tsp dried basil
16 black olives, sliced

1. Roll out each piece of dough and line two 18×27cm (7×11in) baking trays. Leave to rise in a warm place.
2. Soften onion in oil. Drain and divide between trays. Cover dough with tomatoes to within 1cm (½in) of edge. Season.
3. Decorate each tray with anchovy fillets. Sprinkle with cheese and basil. Drizzle remaining oil over filling.
4. Prove in a warm place for 35 minutes. Bake at 200°C (400°F) Gas 6 for 20 minutes until dough is risen and slightly golden at the edges.
5. Decorate with sliced olives. Cut each tray into 16 pizzettes.

Sardine Puffs
Makes 24

6 slices white bread
225g (8oz) (approximately 2 cans) sardines, boned and skinned
1tsp onion, grated
2tbsp lemon juice
225g (8oz) cream cheese
1 egg yolk
½tsp baking powder
Salt
Paprika

1. Remove crusts from bread. Toast one side only.
2. Blend together sardines, onion, lemon juice, cheese, egg yolkes and baking powder. Add seasonings.
3. Spread mixture on untoasted side of bread.
4. Just before serving, grill until puffed and brown. Watch out, as they burn quickly. Cut each slice into squares and serve immediately.

Swedish Meatballs
Makes 36

Delicious with cranberry sauce – buy the best brand you can find.

75g (3oz) breadcrumbs
2tbsp double cream
15g (½oz) butter
½ onion, finely chopped
175g (6oz) beef, minced
100g (4oz) veal, minced
100g (4oz) pork, minced
Salt
Pepper
1tbsp parsley, finely chopped
1 egg, beaten
Oil for frying

1. Mix together the cream and breadcrumbs.
2. Melt butter in a heavy pan. Sauté onion until golden.
3. Combine breadcrumb and cream mixture with minced meat and onion. Add the egg, parsley and seasoning.
4. With wet hands, shape the mixture into meatballs the size of a *small* walnut.
5. Heat the oil. Deep-fry meatballs until brown, for approximately 6 minutes. Drain. Serve warm.

Note: Make in advance, cook and store in the freezer. When required, reheat from frozen in a pre-heated oven, 200°C (400°F) Gas 6, for 15–20 minutes.

Petit Croque Monsieur
Makes 24

12 slices white bread
175g (6oz) ham, sliced
175g (6oz) Gruyère cheese, sliced
175g (6oz) butter, melted

1. Remove crusts and butter bread. Cut each slice in four. Place ham and cheese between slices of bread and make up 24 sandwiches.
2. Pinch edges of bread together.
3. Brush each sandwich with melted butter. Bake in a pre-heated oven, 200°C (400°F) Gas 6, for approximately 10 minutes until cheese melts and sandwiches are crisp and golden.

Index

64